Love Songs

to

My Soul

Poems of Transformation

Jane Granskog, Ph.D.

Love Songs to My Soul

Poems of Transformation

ISBN: 979-8-9918968-0-1

Book Design by Transcendent Publishing
Photography by Jane Granskog

Printed in the United States of America.

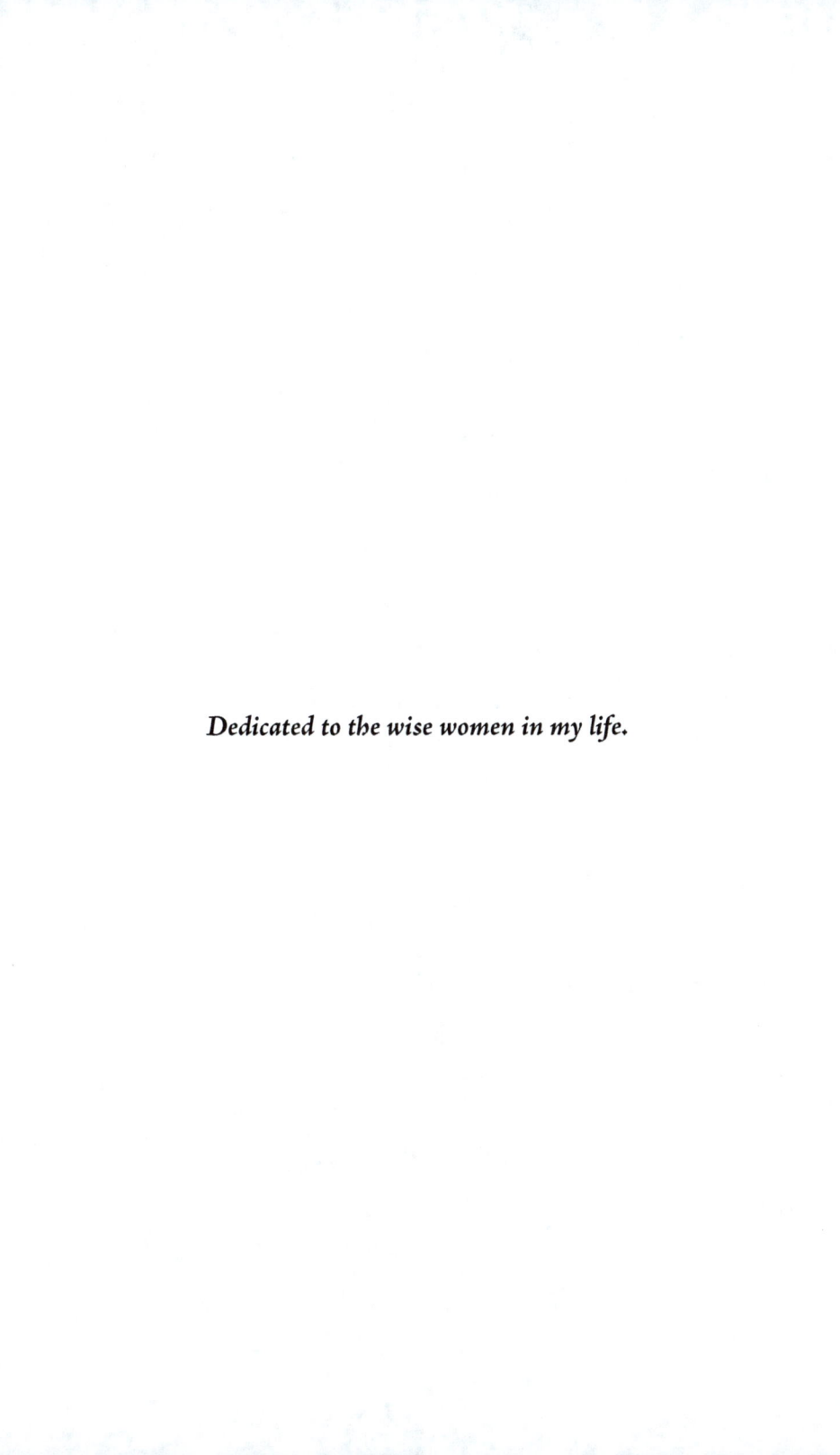

Dedicated to the wise women in my life.

TABLE OF CONTENTS

ACKNOWLEDGMENTS

Poetry has been my heart's voice through the years, and I'm filled with gratitude for the wonderful souls who've nurtured this journey. My deepest thanks go to Shanda Trofe and Transcendent Publishing, whose belief in my work opened the first door, and to her vibrant Author Success Academy community who embraced my verses with open arms.

Dawn Montefusco, you showed me that my words were more than just personal expressions – they were gifts waiting to be shared. Your mentorship lit the path forward when I needed it most.

The Central Coast of California became my muse after retirement, bringing me to extraordinary teachers and communities. Laurie Wagner's Wild Writing group and Deena Metzger's transformative seminars in 2016 and 2019 helped me discover new depths in my writing. At Cuesta College, Sara Roahen, the class instructor along with my fellow storytellers in the Emeritus program helped weave my memories into verse, while the San Luis Obispo Nightwriters taught me to craft my raw emotions into polished gems.

To my beloved friends – Judatha Temple Kline, Laura Lowe, Amelia Aeon Karris, and all the Wise Women in my shamanic and personal circles – your listening hearts and encouraging spirits are etched into every line of these poems. This book carries the echo of your love and support.

PROLOGUE

To All Those I Love

onsidering all the changes we are facing today, not knowing what new event will emerge to startle us awake, how do we keep moving forward with hope? When I look back over the years, I have been putting my thoughts and feelings into words I realized that my life has fallen into three phases.

The first period began in my twenties when I started graduate school. Naïve, and excited at the same time, wondering how to handle myself in a new place – Austin Texas -- I refer to this stage as my maiden years. I found that the naivete I had about my fellow students, as well as the new town and state I was just getting used to, was a bit incomprehensible. From Michigan State University where I had family and friends to the University of Texas in Austin, wow what a journey! That along with my first experience going to Mexico by myself to do a Field School in Cultural Anthropology was both exciting and an overwhelming event. This was especially so, **given that I, as a twenty-two-year-old blonde blue-eyed young woman in the summer of 1968 had little comprehension of the chaos of the times we were going through**.

The second phase began after I received tenure as an associate professor at my first and only job at California State College Bakersfield in the late 1970's. In a department where I was the only female for thirteen years and then only one of two for another five, I struggled to make my voice heard. This was a time I worked with other women throughout the California State University system to bring about an awareness of all the issues we as women faced.

We spoke up and made a difference.

This was also when I discovered my athletic talents, became an Ironwoman triathlete, and used all those difficulties I faced as a woman in my forties in a world dominated by men blasting through to emerge triumphant. My role as advisor and guide to the women students in the courses I taught as well as the student groups which I advised were key to everything I did. I saw this as the "mother" period in my life which continued until past my retirement.

Now I am taking the opportunity to shift my focus to what I can share as a "wise elder woman" with other women about dealing with the challenges of our times. What can I share with other women in all phases of their life about what I went through that might give them strength and understanding to move forward with love?

These are times of change! To know that the next president of Mexico now just newly elected will be a woman. When I think of the confrontations I had with macho men down in Mexico, not acknowledging who and what I stood for and what I did to hold my own presence. Those challenges—recognizing women for more than their bodies-- still exist. The importance of women collaborating to speak up with what we know is the truth of how we feel and what we do—that is the key to a future with hope.

Looking back over the patterns that emerged through these three phases of my life, the set ways that needed to be transformed. I realized that every 15 - 16 years or so, my life has been torn asunder and remolded anew. Each time that it happens, I have used the love songs that flow through me unto the written page to get through to the other side and a new understanding of my path in life.

And it brings to mind what Martin Prechtel said in a workshop I once attended. We need to search out our invisible soul hiding from us in unknown persons and unfamiliar places for it often emerges when and where it is least expected. Our invisible soul wants to be recognized and honored, but we often do not even recognize it when we do see it because our "domesticated" expectations of who and what we have been in the past and what we think we want for the future dominate our perceptions.

I now realize that the common thread that runs through all my poetry is this desire to tease out my invisible soul that I feel and sense in others. It is not so much that I'm looking for someone who will love me for I must learn to love myself first, (although that has certainly been an aspect of my search in the past). What I am really searching for is a kindred spirit, a soul mate with whom to share this life's passage, someone to share the joy of living, the happiness that living life fully in the present brings to each of us.

WEBS

Relationships are akin
to the gossamer filaments
    spiders spin
Delicate threads are they
yet sometimes strong;
moving with the breeze,
geometric shapes
with changing moments......
near, oh so near,
then apart--
torn asunder by
strong gusts of loneliness.

So take care.
Guard them well
to be strong and fine,
catching the dew of dawn,
sparkling with the sun
and thus to remain
always close with one.

    May, 1970
    Austin, Texas

WEBBED REFLECTIONS

There must be spiders to spin
those fine lined filaments
from transient nodal souls,
for there they are:
strands of black despair
spewed from the unaware
and desperate, reaching,
seeking meaning in loneliness;
and fine fuzzy gray products,
of fleeting light in darkness,
limp dead reminders
of a past long gone;
and then
maybe a few
in time anew
of hoped for liquid sun.

Many different shapes
and lengths and strengths--
the mind-etched latticework
of processual spider art?

    June, 1970
    Austin, Texas

···✦✦✦✦✦···

The pain of love is recognition
of the possibility of its absence.

    July, 1970
    San Cristobal, Chiapas

(UNTITLED)

Like a colt I feel now and then;
Curiously aware of all that existing
While prancing in a sunlit glen.
Yet wary I am and ready for running
From those who come to bind and take.
Quietly, cagily, I view they that appear,
Now cautious, now bold, the advances I make;
In youthful yearning drawing near,
Spurting forward, then, suddenly far back.
Distrust of those who seek too much
Grinds with keen need for what I lack.
I search for that shiveringly sensitive touch
Of tamers finely aware and lovingly alive
All the while I'm flitting here and there.
They come, they go. When some arrive
I thrive and grow. They shall know I care.

··✦✦✦✦✦··

Dark green tree-clothed mountains
Shrouded in white cloud tails
Like half-formed fleeting thoughts
Flitting from nowhere to now here
Through the murky mazeways of the mind

And onward -- groping, seeking, reaching --
I travel.

> July, 1970
> San Cristobal, Chiapas

BEGINNING AGAIN

I never thought that I
so scarred and wrought
by fear and pain,
would ever feel quite
like this again:
those golden furiously fluttering
butterflies in me;
that molten mellow yellow
swiftly flowing river
singing in my veins;
that searing sharp fire
piercing my innermost core of being
until I cry from deep inside--
my God, no more!
And it is almost too much you know
for I greatly fear losing
the touch of your sun--
therein lies my pain
in love of you.
It is hard to envision
that such joy was really
meant for lonely me.
And in that, perhaps,
is the key
to what I now feel--
I must pinch myself
to believe that
all this is truly real.

August, 1970
Austin, Texas

THOUGHTS OF YOU

Others may stir my blood,
Kindle my imagination,
Make me smile
Or even laugh in joy.
But only you
Give so much
And to only you
I give my all.

···✦✦✦···

I often wonder
Just how right
All of this is.
And it is
Sometimes still hard
To continue on
Knowing what I do.
But then I feel
That savage exultation
Surging within me --
I know you,
I feel you,
I have you,
I love you.
And nothing else
Really matters.

> September, 1970
> Austin, TX

ON FORBIDDEN LOVE

You enter my mind unbidden
even when I know that
I must put you aside for awhile
to make this aching loneliness
somehow more bearable.
Sober, quiet, almost moody
I pace like a caged tigress
impatient with savage desire.
There is a tightness
strong within me.
It will not depart.
I wish to proclaim
my love of you--
to shout it out loud
until the rafters shake
and echoes ring.
But such is not done.
I cannot do so.
Yet I still shall!
Somehow, in some way, sometime,
I will find the means to fling
this, my gauntlet of love
in the face of the world
that forbids its presence.

September, 1970
Austin, Texas

11

THE PASSING TOUCH

Transient moments
in meetings
charged
with an electric
undefinable.
Finding feeling,
shiveringly sensitive
in a space
too brief
but infinitely long.
It wears
and tears
and shreds
my soul.

Separation does not
negate this bond
so new
so strong
so sought.
Deny a Self
that is myself
in some uncanny way?
Magic of a moment--
it turns my life
upside down
all around.

Ah yes,
I have met
my own
this time?

September, 1970
Austin, Texas

THE SEARCHING

My sister
Where are you?
Now
    when I need you,
Now
    when I feel you
    with such
    strong, smooth-edged,
    binding electricity
My arms are open,
    reaching,
        empty.

And the games continue.
I search murky mazeways
of unknown minds,
guided only by feel;
blind, sensitive--
the too aware with
the touch of too much.

So I seek you.
You,
the embodiment
of empathetic encompassing.
And one day
I just may
uncover who
and what
and where
you are--
to find myself
once more.

        October, 1970
        Austin, Texas

(UNTITLED)

Underground pipelines:
A system of communication
Ruptured, repaired,
To break again
Under stress
In a most unholy way.
Spilling raw reeking
Gut soul torture
Into the causeway
Of an uncaring indifferent tide.

Must we always bottle it up
Until the contents turn foul
With the stench of human misery?

    January, 1971
    Austin, TX

··◆◆◆◆◆··

Where can we go
When peace is nowhere?
Find a friend --
Most anyone will do
To tell your troubles to.
Pour out your heart --
Scatterbrained pain
It won't hurt the telling
Just so you're off and running
Once again.

    September, 1971
    Wichita Falls, TX

LATINA

I am in the sea's tide
Of swarthy, swaggering men
Whose oiled bold eyes roll
Heavenward in drooled
Fancies of night delight,
Of jabbing swollen sticks in
uncaring, tearing, cruel possession.
Because I am WOMAN,
Strange and unknown.
The waters roil, boil—
Steaming fury as my
angered, dismembered, thought-raped
soul recoils from this
sucking, smooth, lewd,
dirt dark tide.
Yet I do surface,
survive still alive for
tendrilled thoughts of HER
coalesce to bathe me in
golden warm, spun soft love.
And I can smile inside,
fighting that tide
with secret strengths
of thought brought gentleness.

San Cristobal, Chiapas, Mexico, 1971

FOR NO REASON

I walk with smiles on my feet
and splash in puddles of sunshine
for no reason
but that my crystal fine web
has the sparkle of dew drops
on warm spun golden strands.

January, 1971, Austin, Texas

WITH YOU IN MIND

Oh yes,
I believe in
golden sun-touched spiderweb
threads extending outward in love.
They close in as filmy words
I weave around and around
surrounding me with their
complicatedness.
To protect me
    (of course)
from you,
love.

···◆◆◆···

We have no words
poetic
when there is
no one to listen.

    June, 1972,
    Santo Tomas, Oaxaca, Mexico

AND THE SEEKING

Fragmented, demented,
Torture trails of thought:
Catagorizing,
Analysing,
Coming up askew,
For the feeling,
Sensing,
Being in
A catatonic frieze,
A frozen figure
Etched against
Naked black sky.
A forlorn soul
Reaching,
Groping,
Clutching
For anything
Knowing it is not touching
Hopelessly
Yearning for dawn --
To be engulfed
In warm sun,
And terribly afraid
Of being
Cold, clean
Sole structure,
Fleshless energy,
As a molecule
In Brownian movement
Arrested
And too aware

Of it's individual existence
Alone
Alone
Alone
In the now
Of timelessness.

June, 1972,
Santo Tomas, Oaxaca, Mexico

RATS

Between tile and cane striped beams
White furry bellies
Darting tailed bodies
So inquisitive, active,
Fearfully cautious,
Unreasonably bold;
Smile bringing these rats,
From my cot below.
    If,
Only if they stay
Amusingly distant,
Like men.

"I"

Time grown giant
Body of memory,
Face of present.
So familiar it is
Punctualized to a node --
Mouth of a swirling
Funnel of "I's"
Sucking in a thousand
More yet unseen,
Swallowed, digested,
Food to grow on
They cycle on forgotten
Leaving only doubtful
Familiarity on return
Surprising experience.

(And my giant just kicked her toe,
Startling my present --
This Jane Doe I just met
Feels like too many others.
    Ouch!!
But stomach smiling food
For all of that.)

    June, 1972
    Sto. Tomas, Oaxaca

(UNTITLED)

Aye but I hunger
For It-only-knows-why-
Or how or when,
With silent keening inside
Awaiting love's essence --
An all consuming sweet muskiness,
The taste of mushrooms,
A soft warm pliable plush cavern,
Fingers exploring velvet
Smooth rounded limbs of strength,
Curves of silence
With long lashed touches of
Intelligent tender understanding.
Quiet now I am (hiding).
But may I yet laugh in gay mischievous
Walking-a-foot-off-the-ground delight
Soon found and always known.

July, 1972,
Santo Tomas, Oaxaca, Mexico

ON DISLOCATION

We are herders
of people herds
and they are herders too.
All of us
forming our identities
on our mismatched herd-mirrors.
Mirrors in mirrors,
as ripples in the water,
cascading mirrors into time,
empty almost
because they are never
exactly right there.

···✦✦✦✦✦···

I keep an entangling web
Of faces in memory.
They are supposed to
Mean something to me.
They do, too, from time to time
When I am in the mood
Of a child lying in the grass
Watching minnows in a brown clear pool.

···✦✦✦✦✦···

Where did she go?
Did you say?
Eh? Can't hear well.
Oh, that a way?
You say?
Ummm, then I'll go
keep on looking.

Got to find her,
sure enough do.
She's me you know.

July, 1972,
Santo Tomas, Oaxaca, Mexico

ON LOVE

Love can be:
  Spy-secret surprise cloaked in night,
New, immediate and overwhelming;
  Mellow yellow soft sun coming
A rosy beginning,
A grand door opening;
  Dew sun touched flowers in sparkling wonder
  With heady mead-sweet delight;
  A gentle warm breeze enveloping
Mischievously light and gay;
  A howling wind, gut tearing strong
With snow-blown exhilaration,
Or sleet driven cold bone reaching hurt;
  Sword whistling sharp dueling
With pain making and taking,
With crimson warm giving,
And sensitive memory scars;
  Grave stones bathed in moonlight bright;
  A long road winding white in unknown dark
From nowhere to ever now here.

Love can be:
  Anything, everything we
  Think, feel and see --
  You and me
  Alive dyingly.

July, 1972,
Santo Tomas, Oaxaca, Mexico

ENCOUNTERS OF A DIFFERENT KIND

Walking off the bus in the Zapotec village in Oaxaca,
surprised me. It was only a two-hour drive from the city.
I wore my blue wrap-around skirt with two big pockets in front.
It was a warm day in May: Mother's Day, 1972.
I was looking for Manuela Galindo.
She was there in the plaza with her youngest, pre-teen daughter, Lydia
And happened to be the very first person I met as I got off the bus.
How was I to know the significance of our encounter?

I had just come from the University of Texas.
Now I had less than a year to finish my dissertation.
Wanted to re-evaluate my life.
Would I get things right this time?

Last time, I spent two years in Chiapas
studying a remote Mayan community.
That trip would take three hours by third-class bus
with chickens on top, and then I had to walk
for another three hours over the mountains
before arriving in the village all alone.
At that time, I had chosen to study
how the people there made a living.

The challenges with men and the patriarchy
was something I was used to in Texas,
but being a single woman in a strange land
made me feel like a nobody.
I never felt I belonged.
This time, I hoped it would be different.

Working with Manuela and her family--the respect we had went both ways.
Washing clothes with others in the river,
Planting maize, beans and squash in the fields.
Accepting the role of godmother to Lydia
We became *comadres*, (co-mothers), acknowledged family.
I offered a celebration to the community—
My Dia de Santo, a blessing in disguise.

I felt connected to all the women there.
They knew everything going on behind the scenes,
Even though men were officially in charge.
I remember how significant their impact was on me

I truly belonged.

>   July, 1972,
>   Santo Tomas, Oaxaca, Mexico

MANUELA

Manuela is
warm brown dappled sun tones
with roots drawn down deep,
slashed and frazzled above,
slightly by seasons turning:
12 children bred, fed, loved
(buried 4, one at life's prime).
Strong, strong, she
withstands life's buffeting winds
with quick sharp tongue-leaves
mercurial movement—
smiling fresh charm at 52.
Now and then she sups
a bit much precious liquid
wanting to forget about
a dead Esperanza of 19,
remembered too well
with tear-filled silent keening.
So she dances—
A majestic willow in gentle
breeze touched sure slowness.
And when too gone to stand unweaving
(no longer touched by the knife edge of pain)
she whispers the all of her:
        "Hablo feo.
        Hablo malo.
        Pero, por Maria Santisima
        Soy yo!"
So she survives,
gnarled and tough,
thread-smooth-worn

and thus, all the more
beautifully, genuinely one.

August, 1972,
Santo Tomas, Oaxaca, Mexico

REFLECTIONS FROM OAXACA

I am as the wind, love,
I cannot stay.
But listen and touch
my ever moving,
ruffling the grass
on the constant changing
skin of the earth
(of which you are a part);
tickling tossing flowers--
just a touch to know and enjoy
and not to let go by;
kicking up autumn colors,
bright delight in sporatic gusts;
and now and then again
winding through tall stately pines
with quiet soothing rustlings
in calm soft notes.
I am here.
Move with me
with care and knowing,
changing ever.
Feel me
with beautifully fierce cold driven snow
reaching in soul-bone deep;
with howling gale anger-hurt
in rafter shaking storming;
with smells of fetid refuse
in tossed off gusts up alley ways,
harsh and pungent;
and with breezed in wafts of wood smoke,
gentle after rain fresh greenness,

and all but scented spring light blooms.
Yes, I am
everywhere in everything.
I gather my soul
with all forms of wind
in mind pictures ageless.
Remember my passing.

August, 1972,
Santo Tomas, Oaxaca, Mexico

WITHOUT SAYING

I reach out --
Nothing.
I act --
One brick,
Two bricks,
A nice solid structure
Invisibly strong;
And react --
Pillage and destroy
To plunder my soul
To seek
To find
To begin
Nothing and everything.

···♦♦♦···

What can I do
with the empty space,
the interstices of words?

With what colors shall I mold
the warp and woof,
the fabric of my being?

Questions without answers
are answered without question
clothed in seamless abstractions.

    October, 1972,
    Santo Tomas, Oaxaca, Mexico

ME VOY

Adonde te vas, mi mujer?
Adonde te vas?
Voy, voy, voy,
No mas que eso, no mas.

Adonde te vas mi mujer,
Adonde te vas?
Voy, voy, voy,
No mas estoy, no mas.

Por qúe me salgas mi mujer?
Por qúe me salgas?
Porque soy, soy yo,
No mas, mujer, no mas.

ROSES AND WIND CHIMES

Yellow roses bloom in snow
nodding gentle to the music--
wind chimes now tinkling soft in blowing breeze--
brass shimmerings in the sun
structured clean and bright
with and against delicate drop-touched velvet
yellow and crystal white
And so my soul speaks
from within calm peace.

Rosas amarillas amanecen
almas frescas respirando
     libre y claro.
Y así estoy yo.
Tocame suave,
delicamente con claridad,
con mi alma lo siento.

These angular bits of brass
tinkle soft in fresh breeze,
jangle sharp harsh in whipping wind--
changing with the flow of moment
yet always constant.

Rosas amarillas amanecen
almas frescas respirando
     libre y claro
Y así estoy yo.
Tocame suave,
delicamente con claridad
Con mi alma te siento

Una amor amanece
rosa y nueva,
> *suavemente.*
Y que hago?
Y que digo?
Nada pero a quedar
> *lleno*
De sabido de alma

Por qúe te lo digo?
Por qúe te ruego?
Por qúe te quiero?
Porque soy yo,
Y sabes que es eso,
No?

February, 1973
Austin, TX

JUST NOW

Pain is strange --
Overwhelming
All over throbbing
For a space non-thinking
Crystal agony
Shivering clear.
And my ego
Screams the night
The everlasting why.

(UNTITLED)

Sleep my darling, sleep.
Into shades of dreaming deep.
In our hands our souls do keep
Fine, fine, the fires leap.

    February, 1973
    Austin, TX

AFTERMATH

The light of the wind caresses me
In scintillating wonder.
Feeling a dappled delight,
A smooth stretching within,
An almost yawn body full,
Soft gentle power
Smoothly unfolding.

···◆◆◆◆◆···

A fragile stem,
A budding bloom,
Bending in tune
With wind blessed caresses.

Wide wondering waves
In weaving lapping grace,
Firm fine sand lace
With sounds softly soothing.

Time touched rocks
Wet with wave action --
Power without mention
In silk strong smoothing.

Gentle, gentle now my love
I give my all to thee.
Gentle, gentle now my love
You give your all to me
Together now in silk soft touch
We let each other be.

April, 1973
Austin, TX

53

PASSION EMERGING

They may call me
a silver tongued devil
(though I am not)
so readily do the words flow
from my mouth.
Yet when I see you,
all my words fail me
caught by the emotional surge
that overcomes me
struck dumb by a blue-eyed angel.

When I see you at a distance
my heart beats wildly,
without rhyme or reason.
And my sense of control,
so finely tuned and
always present within
is no longer there
for the shiveringly aware
oneness with you.
You envelop my soul gently.
Morning glories unfolding in the sun,
only to you do I give my all.

June, 1983
Bakersfield, CA

(UNTITLED)

Tonight as I sit
Listening to crickets
Hoping you will come,
My thoughts are filled
With your presence --
A dew touched rose,
With velvet soft petal skin
All that is beautiful
Without words to define
That is what you are to me.
The minutes tick like hours
And I wait and wait and wait.
Time comes when I can stay no more
And though I know there's reason
The demands of others
(which I know so well)
My insecurities rise to envelop me.
Lost and alone once more I am.

    June, 1983
    Bakersfield, CA

··✦·✦✦·✦✦··

You have been a catalyst
In my life's awakening;
A too oft forgotten sense
Of rightness and harmony with all
That I have always had --
Of who I am,
Where I am at,
And the marvelous beauty of
That which is truly real.

    July, 1983
    Bakersfield, CA

BETRAYED

I am angry!
No -- enraged!
I feel my guts
Spilled out
Oozing raw torture
Opened up by the
Keen blade of emotion.
My life blood
Seeps out over all
And a part of me
Is dying.
I care not --
Spent and wasted,
It matters no more.
How nice to know
People who disappear
When you need the most.
Too afraid to get too close --
It cuts both ways, love.

July, 1983
Bakersfield, CA

ON THE FEELINGS WITHIN

To stand apart,
to objectively isolate
is all too often a
defense against grief,
control against being
opened in pain,
     abandoned and alone.

It is not that you
are unworthy of love
(for in essence
we are all perfectly worthy).
Only that she first asked and
could not openly give.
And the child within,
too young to know it was not her
     closed the door to grief.

The feeling of loss
emotionally driven by
love felt not given.
To control the pain,
the knife turns within
     upon oneself.

··✦✦◆✦✦··

Teacher of the heart,
your kindness in touch,
has come to me
just when I
need it the most.

     September, 1983
     Bakersfield, CA

AWAKENINGS

I feel I ask too much of you
And who am I to do so?
I am not free to give myself
as I would if I only could.
Can I expect anymore of you,
to do and bear what I cannot?
But know this, my love,
what I feel inside for you is real
a soul piercing sweetness that
shall always be within me,
clear, clean through for you
    alone among all.

What I see within you
is what I feel within me--
a quiet, shy vulnerability
clothed with gentle strength;
a sureness of self we all
too often forget we have,
caught in the mad swirl
like a twig twisting hell bent
    down the river of life.

TO A SPECIAL YOU

You are very special
      to me right now
and shall always be.
With you, my love,
I learn to feel again,
exhilaration , joy
      and pain too.
Tocas mi alma
      suavamente.
Lo siento,
      Profundamente.

      September, 1983
      Bakersfield, CA

THOUGHTS OF YOU IN THE AFTERGLOW

My passion rises--
curling light smoke
in early dawn,
unobtrusive at first,
    ignored,
tamped down and out
yet smoldering still
it does not die
    waiting
for the right breeze touch.
It awakens once more--
stoked on feeling,
the flames do leap and dance.
What is this fire within
that takes my will away?
Transformed anew--
burning, bright light
    white heat
I surprise myself
    with my intensity.
And am surprised in turn
    with response in kind.
To share delight, my love,
It is all very right.

    November, 1983
    Bakersfield, CA

SENSING THE NEW

I listen and think,
I feel and probe,
gently in mind:
to learn the essence
to know the you
to find myself.
That is true
experience unfolding,
to merge as one
and still be
uniquely you,
uniquely me,
exploring the wonder,
dappled delight,
touching you within.
It feels so right.

    Aftermath of Veteran's Day
    17 November, 1983
    Bakersfield, CA

ON MY ATTEMPTS TO UNDERSTAND

There is a crying within me.
What is this feeling?
Why is it so intense?
Robbing me of my faculties.
And why this aching inside
of loss and abandonment
which need not be?
Loss of self from Self,
and yet not in truth.
Oh the irony of our
twisted realities, self defined--
convolutions of the soul
we seek to understand.

And I ask you,
    my love.
Did that special, strong feeling
I thought we shared
simply erode away
just like that?
Out of sight, out of mind.
Or is it there still--
hidden behind the barriers
surrounding your soul?

Walls within walls,
we tear them down,
seeking to uncover
the essence of ourselves;
only to discover
them built anew through

remembrance of past lovers.
The past is not now
    My love
And I am not as they.

··•◆◆◆•··

My arms are open
to share a space with you,
here and now without obligation.
For that is all we truly have.
Tomorrow is another day
for untold possibilities
of alternative realities
defined in a future present.
Let not my dreams
of such future possibilities
cloud the reality
of what we may share
together today.

TO YOU

And now it is your turn
How strange.
Sometimes I feel I flit
from one to another
exploring,
seeking,
learning even,
seemingly with a superficial touch
weaving words to screen the feelings
maintaining the distance.

But now I think
I'm falling in love again
It's scary.
And I don't know what to do about it
but to feel as fully as I can
and live the fantasy.

December, 1983
Bakersfield, CA

COMING AROUND FULL CIRCLE

Listening to Melissa's heart songs
my thoughts as always
turn once again to you.
Your mercurial emotions
sliding around and around
heartfelt connections,
questioning the nature of it all.
All these new feelings swirling inside you
a maelstrom of emotion,
bursting out of its bounds.

I feel your energies,
I feel you within me with this
fiery intensity in my heart,
pulsating, vibrating essence.
My Self awakens to
a river of love flowing,
cascading through time and space
to reach out and touch your soul
with rainbow drops of ecstasy
scintillating clean and bright.

And then I stop once more
with an agonizing twist of thought.
Is this connection a one-way flow?
Am I on that lonely road to nowhere
caught in fantasy and despair,
in mind numbing fear of losing
that which might already be gone?
To get past the doubt to the knowing
is always the hardest part.

And yet I must hold on,
remembering exquisite moments:
sharing sunsets over water,
the naked, loving look in your eyes
that touches my soul,
knowing, feeling, this deep attunement within,
the innocence of light and love shared.
Know that you are truly loved
My Love
And that is all that matters.

5 December, 1999

REMEMBERING

Thoughts of running my fingers and lips
over your smooth soft skin,
touching you lightly, sensuously,
kissing you with the velveteen caress
    of rose petals fresh.
You overwhelm my senses
with pregnant potentiality.
With bated breath, my agony lies
in awaiting your response.

    6 December, 1999
    Bakersfield, CA

Belief in fantasy and denial of reality are the stuff out of which deluding dreams and poignant poetry are made.

COMING TO TERMS WITH REALITY

This piercing cold wind
that blows so strong outside
blows within me as well.
Piercing cold hurting within,
numbing the agony of feeling
too much, too deep, too strong

Oh, may it cleanse my soul
of the bone wracking ache
that I feel within
knowing the painful real possibility
of the absence of your
sunshine and love from my life

    20 December, 1999
    Iowa City, IA

MISTS IN TIME

It seems that I
have always known you
even from the first
day that we met.
Familiar patterns of soul
still just faintly felt
not yet with consciousness
knowingly unknowing.
And it has continued such
My sister, my love,
Where does this lead next?

ONCE MORE IT COMES

Quite unexpectedly
with random thoughts that
always come back to you
I am caught in the
shivering throes of emotion
caressing my body entire,
a shimmering electric charge.
Remembering brief moments shared,
just one sidelong glance
from you, it will do.
Awakening an alertness to
that gentle probing feel
a molten, mind etched touch
sensing the connection of soul.

If thoughts of potential possibilities
can bring such an overwhelming loving feel,
a weakness of knees that takes my breath away,
what will such realities made manifest bring?

    February, 2000
    Bakersfield, CA

ONCE MORE FOR LIFE'S UNFOLDING

Symbols and abstractions clothe
My mind, not my heart
But from thinking of you
I cannot depart.
The fineness of light
Springs soft in your eyes.
Your brightness of mind
My own tongue ties.
Your occasional touch
Electrifies with a rush
With overwhelming feeling
My mind turns to mush.

That mush mind focus on feeling is key
You are just the vehicle, you see.
Letting go of machinations of mind for
A heart full of love for everything
Is what truly sets the real me free.

    July, 2000
    Stephenson, MI

ESSENTIAL QUESTIONS

How should I know
that which is true
from delusions of fantasy?
Shall probabilities manifest
from choices past?

Like a bug going this way and that
skittering across the water
unknowingly knowing to
manifest destiny.

How do I now see
that which will last?
How shall I frame
the big picture close up?
Am I afraid of giving voice to remote
probabilities of the impossible achieved?

When will I refrain
from replacing the mask?

Who will find and unfold the secret of
shapeshifting magic into ecstasy?

The Answer:
Finding my Self in myself,
that is my task!

    July, 2000

NOW BLOW

Tendrils of the past
coalesce into the
webs of present,
ensnaring my heart --
a molten blood river red
freeze frozen dried in time.

Oh, may the winds of change
disperse these strands and
free me to love and be
my Self once again.

July, 2000
Stephenson. MI

REFLECTIONS

Patterns of the past
emerge to confront me,
challenge my tranquil security and
lead me to reinvent myself
    once again.
Removing dead husks of the pained past
to bring forth new greenness of
wonder at the beauty of love.
I birth myself anew
with a newfound vision of all.

Only through potential loss
of all that brings meaning and joy
can we travel to the other side
coming through the fire of transformation
    whole once more,
by keeping our essence clear
through the entangling shadows
of what we thought to be real,
straining to find the truth
behind the structures hiding our self from our Self.

And being transformed
brings me the clarity of knowing.
My passion and love of life
reemerges stronger and deeper
    than ever before.
Like the jaguar running silently through the forest,
strong, contained and oh so powerful,
this surging ecstasy of feeling
the energy of the oneness of all
reaches into my deepest core.

I am that I am,
No less, no more.

August, 2000
Bakersfield, CA

PATTERNS REMEMBERED

An ocean of feeling overwhelms me,
cascading in glistening waves,
enveloping my body entire.
All this from
the mere thought of you.
The cultured texture of your voice
lies at the base of my awareness as
thin tendrils of smoke and fire
surrounding my heart in loving tones.
I delight in the light
of your warm soft brown eyes,
and melt at the mere scent
of your presence in my mind.
The intelligence of your soul spirit
is one I have always known
but thought long lost in
vast eternities of time.

I have been searching for you
all my life, you know.
Catching brief patches of patterns
reflected in those who seemed to fit
but then again not.
Patterns of light on the forest floor,
mingling with the shadows of
an almost memory trace.
Layering leaves of experience
covered up the moist womb earth
and the grief of your leaving so soon.

And still my mind questions on
the feel of this reality.
My Self reflected as my Self?
Can this really be?

    27 August, 2000
    Bakersfield, CA

ENCOUNTERS OF A THIRD KIND

My feelings for you
have not changed, my love.
They have only become
more resonantly sound and
fine tuned in time
singing my heart awake.
Still complexity weaves in
more twists and turns each day
bringing faint scented nuances
to new formed relationships.
Moon flowers unfold in the
full light of the night
as that which is left unsaid
grows more palpably rich
with each passing moment.

And dewdrops on my
warm spun spider strands
are kissed by the sun again
all because I have
opened my heart to love.

···◆ ◆ ◆ ◆···

A rich red Merlot
maturing in oaken casks
in time, fine wine
emerging clear with
a poignant delicate bouquet.
And so too
with the two of you.
trust, affection and love

singing in the heart
comes forth in due time
encased in the strength
and knowing in the bones.

13 October, 2000
Bakersfield

AND YET AGAIN. . .

It is not something
to be figured out
or so I tell myself
as I keep on trying
to figure us out.
What is this connection
that takes my breath away,
leaving my thoughts
suspended in space
and that makes my heart sing
with the fullness of sun's heat?
The touch of your Soul is
scored deep in the recesses
of my Soul/Spirit/Mind
that timeless bedrock of eternity --
always present, ever known.
But in the conscious awareness
of this fragile self I am here,
traces of waves in the sand
only faintly remembered still.
And the forever question
pregnant with hope and love
wiggles its way to awareness.
Can this possibly be real?
To find my heart and soul's desire
full fleshed right in front
of my newly opened eyes?
How do I believe in that
which I only think I see?
I just must trust in
what I really do know,
to let things unfold,
to be and grow.

13 November, 2000
Bakersfield, CA

97

WITNESS

Owl peers out from
her cottonwood branch
overlooking the river with
quiet waters flowing.
Silent witnesses
to my unspoken thoughts,
posing the questions within.
Listen carefully and you will hear
the thundering of the universe
in the murmuring of water
smooth flowing over rock,
letting no barrier
impede its passage.
Oh that I may find my answers in
the quiet strength of river rocks
feeling the gliding rush of water
flowing forever free
through and over me.

And you too are my witness,
standing there quietly with
that lovingly alive look.
Observing, clarifying
with a minimum of words,
mirroring to me
that which I need to see,
sketches of an inner design,
the scapes of my Being.
Getting me to listen to
the touch of my heart.
Reaching out to all around

and fully feeling
the bliss of Love.
Only in the thunder of silence
do I truly knowingly feel
the dancing of my Soul
in sacred rhythm with you and all.

So teach me, my love
to dance forever free
and thus to feel and be
fully authentically me.

Bakersfield, 23 November, 2000

HERON

Beautiful blue gray heron
perching on one leg
bridging earth and sky
centered and still
as life waters flow by.
Help me to stay so
balanced and true,
to follow my heart
as I know I must do
with focused awareness
on that which is really here.
My path shall unfold
and all will be clear.

26 November, 2000
Bakersfield

PONDERING ON THE ILLUSIONS OF REALITY

Sometimes ...
far, far too often
it seems as of late,
my desire for you
is so fierce and intense
I can hardly contain myself.
I want you in my arms
to devour you with my passion
that knows no bounds.
Even the mere thought of
an ecstatic union with you
invites visions of exploding
galaxies of white light
flooding every cell of my being.
And my sense of Self
expands without bounds
filling the universe with love.
I have to force myself back
weak kneed and limp
to return to the constraints
of this reality I now face.
Struggling to maintain the
transpersonal stance of healer,
sister and friend to you
becomes harder and harder to do.
So I say to myself:
take several deep breaths,
go out on a walk,
do what you must
to sustain the trust.
Don't push the river

all in good time
waiting a bit longer
is not such a crime.
Maybe you are not even
the one I've been waiting for
all my whole life long.
After all, I know it's not the
first time I've been wrong.
Look at all those who came before.
Besides, you never have said
how you really feel about me.
Innuendoes and looks and
an occasional touch
are all I have to go on
and that isn't much.
Perhaps the connection with you
I so strongly feel
is but an illusion,
a one-sided fantasy
created out of frustrated desire
or remnants of lifetimes past
and not at all real now.
And I try to tell myself again:
you have to block it all off,
close your heart down,
and keep the boundaries intact.
Don't let anyone know
how you're bleeding inside.
Smile, be cool,
stay self contained,
detached and restrained.
Just let it all go on and
stop trying to figure it all out.
All these words help

to keep me sustained
for a while at least
until the agony of my ache
to be with you again
breaks to the surface once more.
My heart seems to expand so
when I am with you
just from the sheer pleasure
of your presence
I feel I know way
deep down to my core
you are the one I've been waiting for.
So how much longer
is my everlasting cry?
In frustration sometimes I just
want to shut down and die,
crawl in a hole and
let the whole world go by.
I need only to remember
that refrain echoing in my brain:
Stay open to Spirit
to guide you to what's true
only with an open heart
will you know what to do.

December, 2000, Bakersfield, CA

HAVE I TOLD YOU LATELY?

Have I told you lately
just how much I love you?
That my thoughts always seem
to turn effortlessly to you with
but the subtlest of reminders?
It is the faintly familiar stance
of a stranger seen from afar,
or the soothing sound of water
murmuring in the fountain,
the whisper of wind through the trees.
Everything seems to remind me of you.
and my mind is flooded
with the memory of all
those special brief moments
we have shared together.
Whenever I am near you,
my heart fills with ecstasy
and I feel the fullness of our
minds melding in an everlasting now.

January, 2001

TO MY BELOVED

May the sun always kiss you
with its warm brilliance.
May the waters of life
flow through and around you
washing away all that takes away
from manifesting the marvelous
woman that you truly are.
And may the joyous music of the universe
always fill your heart with healing sounds
allowing you to fully express
the beauty you offer to all.

January, 2001

ON THE UPS AND DOWNS OF LIVING AND LOVING

There have been those moments again
catching me unprepared as of late
when the dank, dark, black clouded
stillness of a moonless night
permeates my forlorn soul
all from the mere thought of
the absence of your presence
in my life and in my heart.
When I ask myself the agonizing
inevitable questions of loss and despair:
Who do I think I am fooling?
What do I think I am doing?
Will the angst of my desire
finally quietly fade away
leaving an empty hollow acceptance
of the inevitability of fate displaced?
Yet I am not one to succumb
to a destiny not of my making.
In the core of my being, I know
the depth and strength of our connection
is a heart strong bond of love and light
that transcends both time and space.
Mother, sister, lover, mate,
you have been and are all of these
to me, my friend, and so much more.
And it is that innermost knowing
that keeps me anchored and strong
when the winds of desolation
attempt to blow me off course.
So I take a deep breath and
remember to hold onto the light

the fiery spirit that burns within
entwining our hearts and embracing our souls
as we do this healing work together.

March, 2001

JUST BEING

As I sit here quiet
my senses open full out
embracing the sounds, smells and
loving light feelings that
thoughts of you
always bring to me
I am struck once again by
the strength of our bond.
To stop or change the way
I feel about you is to
ask the sun not to rise
and spread its life-giving force
over the world anew each day;
to dam all the rivers
so they no longer
flow back to the sea.
And I am beginning to realize
the underlying essential truth:
as I know how to swim,
I know how much I love you.
And in the process
I remember my Self.

March/April, 2001

THE IVY EFFECT

I really didn't expect
so very much, you know
when you first said
that ivy in the relationship
corner of my yard
just had to go,
strangling the tree that way
with its entangling green vines.
How could I possibly see
through the entanglements
of my own life with
that in my yard?
I knew it was true
the next step I had to take.
I didn't much contemplate
its meaning and effect on me.
I just knew it was something
that together, we'd do.
But the joyous exultation I felt
tearing those vines away with you,
letting all the sun shine through
and feeling so gloriously free,
to so fully authentically be,
that was surprising to me.
My heart bursts full with joy
at your wonderful gift of love
and I feel so very blessed
to have you in my life.
You have helped me to
remove my blinders and see.
I had never paid much attention before

to what I was really doing,
how giving my life force
to those that I loved,
ignoring the ivy's growth so long,
could take me so far away
from my true path to Self
while shrouding me all around
in a green wall of denial.

And I still have to admit
I feel very exposed,
vulnerable to the sun's rays
clear and free for all to see
like a newly washed raw rock
in Spring's river melt.
Yet this much I know:
accepting love from
a woman I love is a
most precious place to be.

April, 2001

LISTENING TO HAWK

Oh Red tailed Hawk
flying so bold and free,
what is it that you
are trying to say to me?
Flashing your bright red tail,
swooping in front of my eyes,
I can only surmise
kundalini rises and I must awake.
Prick up my ears and listen,
be ready for the slightest cues.
Oh help me see my way clear
through entangling illusions and lies
and not fall prey to others' views.
For I cannot do anything
about what others think
of who I am and what I do.
I can only stay true to
the Divine essence within:
express my passion and love for all,
flying with you on winds of faith,
that wondrous spirit that
surrounds me round,
lifting and blessing my way.
For only when I truly do so
will I walk my talk
with fullness of heart
and the serenity of peace and joy.

May 2001

DRAGONFLIES DANCE

Sitting on my favorite rock
on a very special day in June
down by the river flooded full
from spring mountain rains.
Pondering beginnings and endings
of that which needed letting go,
events of present now past,
lessons learned of love and loss.
Contemplating the mystery of now
while not really thinking at all.
Deadwood flotsam bumps along
past new green cattail stalks
as snowy egrets rise startled
touching me with their graceful flight.
My thoughts are like that,
bumping away until startled awake.

And I am caught by the dance of dragonflies,
Cavorting right in front of me.
They delight in flight, here and there,
bright red lace webbed wings outstretched,
pausing on slender cattail blades,
begging my attention, they tantalize
my awareness now keenly alert
for provocative meanings.
What is it that I do now know?
What truly is or what may be?
That hope may ride on fickle winds
while faith endures dark
storms of doubt and fear?
And it must be that to You I turn

for in hands of the Mistress Divine
fate spins webs star flung fine.

Trust in the power of light and love
the dragonflies dance for me
I've done the work and now it is
indeed my time to shine.

June/July, 2001

AWAKENING THE SPIRIT WITHIN

Reflecting on the possible probable
listening to words of foresight
given on request from
the stones, stars and cards,
spirit unfolding before me
all for my knowing and becoming.
Awakenings of a different kind
new consciousness emerging
knowing, feeling, sensing,
my twin flame burning
with imposed distance yearning
but only for the time being.
Just as Great Horned Owl
flies silently through the night
in a warrior stance of love and light
watching and quietly waiting
for shadows of doubt and fear
to disappear in starlight bright
as yet another pattern is born.
Fine spun filaments unfolding
with new networks, fate made
and only occasional unwelcome
lapses of synapses,
those disruptions of flow
when doubt and fear creep back in --
my attempts to push the river
when I know not where it goes.
But that is also precisely when
the words of the Mistress Divine
return most clearly in my mind:

Let go and trust in the power
of the Great Goddess, Kwan Yin within
for only then, will I true love find.

October, 2001

SPEAKING MY TRUTH

In searching for myself
I have struggled to speak
myself into existence
fearing that those that I love
will disappear once again
if I don't say who I am
over and over and over
until I, too, believe it to be true.
But when I get past all that,
realizing it is indeed
my own story I create,
that all the rest are
only secondary characters
in my fable of the truth that is,
and finally connect with the
beautiful Being I truly am,
there will be no more
need for words for
I decide, my story, my truth,
without doubt, of who I really am.

November 2001

THE DANCE

There is a delicate dance we do,
you and I, with words unspoken,
back and forth, never too close
while breathing synchronicity
in felt mental merging.
I hesitate and pause,
unsure of my bearings
crossing over the bridge of connection,
afraid I may misstep and fall
engulfed by the swift moving river below,
smashing to smithereens on
resisting rocks of indifference,
sucked down by currents of
betrayal not mine to express,
abandoned and lost by designs unknown.
Questioning all for the reality fit,
starting, stopping, asking once more,
are you part of my destined fate?
Or am I making more than what is?
Perhaps this relation is not meant
to be any more than what now exists.
And yet I still feel the very strong pull
your light love energy opens in me.
Drawn to dance forward once more,
as I watch you move so carefully back
keeping those boundaries clear and intact,
well-guarded fences, private holdings of Soul
your council of Self contained, undisclosed.
So what is it you mirror, I don't
wish to see reflected back in me?
And what do I mirror back to you in truth?

That boundaries so defined do hold the key
to true empowerment of the essential Self?
It is I realize, a gift of real reciprocity,
that in our gentle, now joyful dance
we define the ground to let each other be.

March 2002

SISTER SPIRITS

Three soul sisters we are,
Sandra, Paula and I
traveling our way from afar,
as unknown distant threads
now newly woven together
in telling tapestry patterns
three days in the making –
a gathering of women in Oregon.
The sharing of stories unfolded
women healing life's lesions of
abandonment, abuse, and despair,
finding voice to expose the wounds
so mother, daughter, sister, Self
can be made whole once more.
The Goddess in her many forms
laughingly brings in light and joy
to the potentiated dark of before.
Spirit Guides transcending.
Black wolf nurtures and protects,
when needed is always there.
Mother Bear's enduring strength
hibernating winter to reflect,
now spring awakened cubs to grow
as hummingbirds of paradise
dance among the daffodils.
And spiraling snakes transform
healing wisdom from past pain.
Interwoven threads of meaning
shaking in empathic feeling
brings forth the love we share.
Above all, this is for Paula

with heart filled joy and gratitude
we honor what she has endured.
Her story brought to light
imaged vision of body scars
mapping the roads of pain
endured and survived.
We as witnesses to strength in sharing,
healing the wounds of womanhood.
Paula, you bless us with your presence.

March, 2002

HEART OF THE MATTER

Home is where the heart is, or so they say.
What happens when the heart is broken?
Feeling displaced, searching to belong:
smashed down, snapped open.
Cracked like an egg to get to the yolk.
Or the seed pushing through the hard shell in
the darkness of soil to the light above.
So, too, I remind myself, tomorrow
is a new day yet to be exposed,
and then to be embraced and held
in the strength of new beginnings.

April 2018

ONE MORE REFLECTION ON LOVE

One more reflection on love
A four-letter word expressing what we long for
To be in deep fulfilling relation to each and all.
So now, what does that require?
The feelings manifesting each day anew.
To walk easily up past the houses on the dirt trail
To where the live oaks cluster.
Solid trunks stretching out parallel to the ground
then reaching up to frame the sky.
A place where I can sit back and embrace
The beauty and stillness of just being here.
The trees, the sun, the rain now gently falling
Each so needed to continue for the living.
All this and more.
Today I am in love with
full hearted appreciation and gratitude
for all that I am gifted to witness
Free to be me, this time, this place
Right here, right now!

And yet, I cannot help at the same time
remembering, noticing, experiencing being here
is also to grieve the loss of all that is no longer.
The extinction of species, all we have lost
through the disconnect from our Mother.
Me, mine, us, them – how we have othered
anyone different, human and non-human.
Consuming, ravaging the earth with no thought
of the eventual collapse of all that we take for granted,
what we thought would continue as before.
So, I hold both the grief and pain at what is lost forever

with the joy and celebration of what I witness here.
Free to be me, this time, this place
Right here, right now!

May that impel me to action,
going forth to make a difference in what I say and do
and hold forth the possibility of a different Earth
sustained in harmony and balance, loving life and All that is.

January, 2019
Los Osos, CA

SPIRIT SPEAKS

Spirit speaks in the rustling of wind
through the branches of Grandmother Big Pine,
and in the almost invisible web strung next to her trunk,
interwoven threads of meaning spun by Orb spider.

Quietly asking this one to listen,
listen within, listen without.
Pay attention to the signs.
See with new eyes, hear with your heart.

Speak the truth of what is.
The wind blows soft, then strong.
The spider spins webs from her belly.
The trees stand solid, branches moving in place.

Afraid to step forward, thinking no one will listen.
Hearing Spirit say, speak heartfully anyway,
loud enough to catch their attention,
soft enough so they'll ask for more.

Though it seems impossible, still I shall.
Staying in the mystery of Presence,
without knowing how or when or what,
I give it up.

> June, 2019
> Topanga Canyon, CA

BETWEEN LIGHT AND SHADOW

Between light and shadow
what lies in wait for what?
Light is what comes in with an aha.
Shadow is what crosses my mind
with grief at what appears to be gone
or at least in a place not easily seen.
What shadows remain behind me
when I face the light of day?
The new way of being here now
Letting the shadows pass away.
As the grief at what is lost
lies forgotten in the dark
Only to come back anew
when memories of the past
emerge once again,
when the thought of what's lost
jumps up alight in my mind.
Oh, may I find the way
to balance the light and shadow,
knowing both are necessary truths,
breathing once again and letting go
to know what truly lies in my heart.

12 Oct., 2020

WHEN DAY BECOMES NIGHT

When the day becomes night
and I reflect on what I've done.
How quickly the day has disappeared
just as the tasks before me
slip away like the silent pace of the jaguar
smoothly gliding through forest.
Meditating on what has transpired
What I've done and what I've left.
To sleep now with more for the morrow
When once again I gather up what's inside
ready to face when night turns to light.
Dreams of a new and different day
will my tracks follow a new path?

October 21, 2020

THIS I AM

I am a woman of the woods.
I walk through the trees,
down along the river
my spirit guides by me.
Deeply rooted in the earth,
strongly centered and whole
I follow my path and I know where to go.
I am that I am and I know what to do.
Teacher/healer is my path
balanced and true.

I am a weaver of worlds, here and afar
indigenous knowing learned, patterns I share.
To stand up for those of the earth left behind
and to give voice to injustices wrought
I speak truth to power to bring forth
the gifts of grassroots action sought.

I am a healer of hearts
with the heat in my hands I note
the threads of both joy and pain
finding the ways to weave them together again
into a newfound presence of Being

A spiritual warrior woman present now here
strong as a bear I know how to persevere.

The light of my soul shines strong and bright
as I speak with heart what I feel is right.
To share stories of mine and those I reach,
I listen within, all senses alert

for the wisdom of the ancients coming through
with words of wise council.
I share what I feel and know to be Truth
in all its many guises.
With clarity, focus, ease and grace,
I guide each home to their rightful place.

I AM THE ONE

I am the One
who hears the voice within.
I am the One
who speaks truth to power.
I am the One
who listens to my body.
I am the One
who takes time for myself.
I am the One
who carries the solution.
I am the One
who spends time writing my truth
I am the One
who asks for support when I need it.
I am the One
who is here to break old patterns.
I am the One
who accepts that which I am
I am the One
who is responsible for all my life experiences.
So be it and so it is.

November 18, 2020

ABOUT THE AUTHOR

Jane Granskog, Ph.D., taught cultural anthropology at CSU Bakersfield for 38 years, researching indigenous Mexican tribes before retiring in 2012. A lifelong poet, she has used verse to express her authentic self throughout her vibrant life. Granskog's diverse passions led her to complete over 120 endurance events, including the Ironman World Championship, and explore spiritual and shamanic practices. Her research on women triathletes over 40 culminated in the book, *Athletic Intruders: Ethnographic Research on Women, Culture and Exercise.* As an elder woman anthropologist, Granskog weaves together her experiences as a teacher, athlete, and spiritual seeker to guide others on the "path of the wise woman." Her journey, chronicled through both academic work and poetry, reflects her quest for self-discovery and her desire to help others find their authentic selves.

Contact: Jane@IronWomantoWiseWoman.com